Collies at Work

Sabrina Lakes

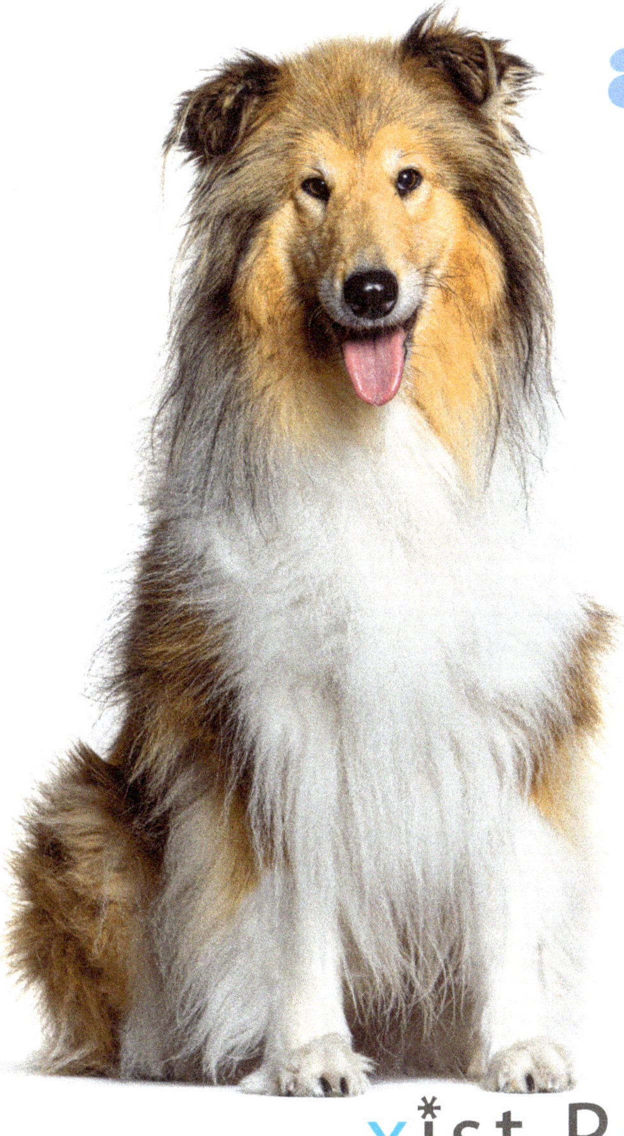

x*ist Publishing

Check out all of the books in the Paws and Pastures Series

Published in the United States by Xist Publishing
www.xistpublishing.com
© 2025 Copyright Xist Publishing

All rights reserved
No portion of this book may be reproduced without express permission of the publisher.
All images licensed from Adobe Stock

First Edition
Hardcover ISBN: 978-1-5324-5543-8
Paperback ISBN: 978-1-5324-5544-5
eISBN: 978-1-5324-5542-1

PUBLISHED IN TEXAS

Table of Contents

Introduction to Australian Shepherds	2
Fun Facts About Australian Shepherds	5
What is Herding?	6
Why Australian Shepherds are Great Herders?	9
Training an Australian Shepherd	10
Games to Help Australian Shepherds Learn	12
A Day in the Life of a Working Australian Shepherd	14
Working with the Animals	17
Caring for an Australian Shepherd	19
Keeping Your Australian Shepherd Healthy	20
Australian Shepherds at Rest	22
Fun Activities for Australian Shepherds	24
Glossary	26
Index	27
Keyword List	28

Meet the Collie

Collies are medium-sized dogs. They have long fur and a slim body. They come from Scotland. Farmers used them to help with animals. Collies are smart and gentle. They love to play and work hard. There are many different kinds of Collies.

Fun Facts About Collies

Collies are very energetic. They can run fast and jump high. Collies have beautiful fur that comes in different colors. Their ears can stand up or be folded. Many people love Collies because they are so loyal.

What is Herding?

Herding means guiding animals like sheep or cows. Collies help farmers keep animals in groups. They move the animals to new places. This job is very important on farms.

Why Collies are Great Herders

Collies are great herders because they are smart. They learn quickly and follow orders. Their long legs help them move fast and cover large areas. Collies are also very brave and strong.

Training a Collie

Training a Collie is fun and easy. Start with simple commands like "sit" and "stay." Use treats to reward good behavior. Be patient and kind. Collies love to learn new things.

Games to Help Collies Learn

Games make training fun for Collies. Play fetch to teach them to come back. Hide treats and let them find them. This helps them use their noses and brains. Another game is herding a ball, which is like herding animals.

A Day in the Life of a Herding Collie

Collies start their day early. They eat breakfast and get ready. Then, they help the farmer with the animals. They guide the sheep or cows to the fields. Collies are always busy.

Working with the Animals

Collies work hard all day. They keep the animals together and safe. They run around and make sure no animals get lost. Collies use their barks and nips to move the animals. They are very good at their job.

Caring for a Collie

Collies need good food to stay strong. They eat healthy meals twice a day. Brushing their fur keeps it shiny and clean. Collies also need their nails trimmed regularly. This helps them walk and run better.

Keeping Your Collie Healthy

Collies need exercise every day. Walks and playtime are important. They also need check-ups at the vet. This keeps them happy and healthy. Collies love to be active and busy.

Collies at Rest

After working hard, Collies need rest. They like to nap in cozy spots. Resting helps them recharge for the next day. Collies also enjoy cuddling with their owners.

Fun Activities for Collies

Collies love to play, even when they are resting. They enjoy toys that squeak or bounce. Puzzle toys keep their minds busy. Spending time with their family makes them happiest of all.

Glossary

Check-up A visit to the vet to make sure a pet is healthy.

Commands Words or signals used to tell a dog what to do, like "sit" or "stay."

Exercise Activities like walking or playing that help keep a dog strong and fit.

Grooming Taking care of a dog's fur and nails to keep them clean and healthy.

Herding Guiding and moving animals like sheep or cows.

Nip A small, quick bite used to move animals.

Recharge Resting to get energy back after working or playing.

Treats Special food given to dogs as a reward for good behavior.

Index

animals 5, 2, 7, 13, 14, 17
body 2
brains 13
colors 5
commands 10
cows 7, 14
dogs 2
ears 5
farmers 2, 7
Work 1, 3

Keyword List

Nouns	Verbs	Adjectives	Adverbs
animals	come	beautiful	always
body	eat	brave	early
brains	find	cozy	quickly
collie	follow	gentle	regularly
colors	guide	long	together
commands	have	loyal	very
cows	help	medium-sized	
dogs	jump	slim	
ears	keep	smart	
farmers	learn	strong	
farms	move		
fields	play		
fur	rest		
jobs	run		
meals	stand		
owners	start		
scotland	teach		
sheep	use		
treats	work		

www.ingramcontent.com/pod-product-compliance
Ingram Content Group UK Ltd.
Pitfield, Milton Keynes, MK11 3LW, UK
UKHW050147010425
456966UK00004B/23